Autism IS My Superpower

A Parental Guide to Accepting Your Child's Au-someness

Tracie Green

Foreword

Resilience: It is something I've always admired about my sister—her ability to recover quickly has consistently been one of her strengths. This quality sets her apart from everyone else. Although this journey was not easy for her, she toughed it out and faced all the challenges head-on. Despite encountering numerous obstacles, she never folded or gave up on herself, her husband, or her children. Life dealt Tracie a hand she wasn't sure she could fully handle, but she chose to stay in the fight. She chose to walk her path to find her purpose and didn't stop until all her questions were answered. I have watched her numerous times break down, get up, pull herself together, and readjust her crown every time. She was determined to make the best out of the hand life dealt her. As a big sister, it makes me proud to see my baby sister walking with her head held high. I am even more proud to see that she has navigated this journey so well that her children are turning out to be as amazing as she desired them to be.

When you look at Tracie's children, you see that they are the product of her hard work coming full circle. You witness their dedication playing out in the best way, and you see how confident and bold they are for such little individuals. The person, woman, wife, and mother she is today, many doubted she would become, but she has gracefully transitioned into her role. I have always believed in Tracie, but now she believes in herself; she needed that! She has flourished into the person I always knew she would be, and her resilience is now at an all-time high.

-Cecily Landown

Special Dedication

To our beautiful creations, my blessings, our greatest gifts from God: Tristan, Kameron, and Aaliyah. You three are my reasons to keep going in this life. I never knew a love so pure until I was blessed with the three of you.

Tristan, I didn't give you the gift of life, life gave me the gift of you, and it is one of the best gifts I could ever imagine, the best gift I could ever open. Being your bonus Mom has been nothing short of amazing. Everything started with you. This journey belonged to you and me before it belonged to all of us. I want to say to you, thank you! Thank you for coming into my life and making everything so bright and colorful. Thank you for being my first teacher on this Au-some journey.

We didn't know it then, but you were preparing me for something I had no clue about; you opened my eyes to great possibilities. You were my first child and my first son. We have been through it all together. My heart is yours just as much as it is your siblings'. We aren't blood, but I don't need blood to define the love I have for you nor the bond we built from the time we met until this very moment in our lives. I love you more than life itself, and I pray that you always know and feel that.

Kameron, you are the sun that lights up the sky. You are so full of joy and light that it's hard not to watch you shine. You are my first-born son, my initial realization of parenthood, and from the moment you took form in my womb, I sensed you were destined for something extraordinary. Your arrival was unexpected yet perfectly timed; I didn't comprehend how much I needed you until you were in my arms. My heart swelled with love, and every moment spent with you became a cherished memory.

You are a child of God, destined for greatness, and your potential knows no bounds in this world that is yours to explore. Thank you for being precisely what Mommy needed, unapologetically embracing your fearless, strong-minded, and brave nature at such a tender age. You hold countless remarkable qualities, and I am confident that as you mature, you will evolve into an even more remarkable individual. Despite being a middle child, your protective instincts make you seem like the eldest, and I appreciate your role as a leader among your siblings. I love you immensely, and I pray that God continues to shower blessings upon your life. May you follow the path of Christ and be a beacon to others.

Introduction

I never thought I would be on a journey like this one, but now that I am, I feel that it's necessary for me to share my story with others, especially after overcoming many trials and triumphs in the last few years of my life. My mother-in-law, among many others, suggested that I speak out to help guide other parents who may be facing similar struggles or challenges that I have encountered on this journey.

On September 15, 2022, I decided to take my mother-in-law's advice and began creating inspirational reels on Facebook and TikTok to share with other Mothers about the journey I am on. I received a plethora of positive feedback as well as a multitude of questions. It took a while, but finally, on November 20, 2022, after a long talk with my mother-in-law and prayer, I decided to move forward with telling my story. I was grateful that so many people believed in me.

I've struggled with finding my purpose, and at first, I thought writing a book was out of my league. Doubts lingered in the back of my mind, but I stayed on course and began to write. Discouragement tried to set in throughout this process concerning support and finances, but I did not waver; I kept pushing. There were times when I wanted to give up, but I was reassured that my children's journey and mine would inspire others.

I overcame exhaustion, stress, sleepless nights, and many emotional battles within myself. I realized that if I could make it through that with my head held high, then giving up wasn't an option. I'm praying to touch the lives of many Mothers and Fathers who may be battling this life-changing journey. During this journey, you must persevere. Don't allow the devil to discourage you from unlocking new levels of greatness in your life or your children's lives. Allow yourself to travel this journey with a clear heart, a settled spirit, and an open mind full of endless possibilities.

Writing this book, along with the encouragement from family and friends, has helped me understand myself as well as other mothers with journeys similar to mine. My family and friends have helped build up my spirit, courage, confidence, and willingness to speak about my story. Listening to their uplifting words inspired me to step out on faith and fulfill my purpose.

I often wondered what my calling might be in life. I never thought it would be writing a book to inspire others, but I am passionate about the journey I am on. I want to help those around me as well as others, if possible, by sharing knowledge that I had to find on my own or learned through experience. I want other Moms to see how far I've come on my journey and be inspired to stay the course, to walk by faith and not by sight when it seems to be getting hard, to always remember that there is a rainbow after every storm, and that they are not walking alone on this journey. I, along with many others, am walking with you, and we are going to get through this one beautiful puzzle piece at a time.

-Tracie Green

Chapter 1

Mommy, I'm Unique

Have you ever looked at your child(ren) and sensed that something was different? Not different in a bad way, but in a unique way? When my bonus son was around 11 months old, I observed a subtle change in him. It wasn't overt; rather, it was a nuanced shift that I picked up on. I like to call it "bonus Mom intuition". Having been with him since he was 3 months old, I knew him quite well, and the bond we created was beautiful. He had always been such a happy, relaxed, and laid-back baby, but as he grew older, something about him stood out to me. The first signs of his uniqueness became apparent in the way he would have tantrums. Despite not being a biological Mom at that time, I had some experience with children as an aunt and had also worked in childcare for a while after high school. I had witnessed my share of tantrums, but there was something about the way he had them that alarmed me. When I discussed it with my husband, he brushed it off as normal, thinking it was part of typical behavior. However, my bonus Mom intuition persisted.

Over time, I noticed the disappearance of the words he used to say, setting off another alarm in me. I never entertained the thought that he could be on the spectrum, as I lacked knowledge about it and had not encountered any children on the spectrum before. I simply felt he was progressing at his own pace, understanding that all children are different and uniquely special. He also developed into a picky eater, particularly disliking fruits and vegetables. While not uncommon, I didn't find it alarming, thinking it was a typical phase. It was only after he turned one, now a newfound big brother to our second-born son, that I discovered just how unique he was. To ensure he didn't feel left out with the new addition to our family, I engaged in various activities for one-on-one time. Arts and crafts became my go-to for bonding time.

One day, I decided to use cute little pom-poms with him, and he was completely terrified at the sight of them; that was mind-blowing to me. Not only was he afraid of the pom-poms, but he was also afraid of feathers, cotton balls, leaves, and spikey balls. It was interesting to me because I had never experienced a child being afraid of items that weren't harmful, and it was always just the sight of them that would terrify him. He would be running, screaming, and shaking as soon as he saw either item around the house. It came to a point where we would hide the cotton balls so he wouldn't see them, as well as get rid of any arts and crafts items that would terrify him because we didn't want him to become traumatized by these items.

Eventually, we decided to take him to the eye doctor to get his eyes checked out, ensuring he wasn't seeing anything other than the actual objects at hand. The eye doctor stated that his vision was fine, but he could possibly be seeing things in a different way. He was prescribed glasses to see if they would help with how he viewed the items of which he was afraid. However, it didn't work at all. He would still be terrified at the sight of those objects. At that point, I knew our son was unique. Being unique means being the only one of your kind, unlike anything or anyone else. Uniqueness comes from within and is expressed through our actions and behaviors. I consider it a true blessing to be the parent of unique children; my bonus son isn't our only unique child. We welcomed our first daughter in 2020, born at 31 weeks and 5 days gestational; she was a preemie. She entered the world perfectly, weighing 3 lbs. 5 oz. Due to her premature birth, our daughter was expected to reach developmental milestones a little later than children born at full term.

I recognized her uniqueness from the moment she arrived; she was strong-willed and a fighter. It came as no surprise when she met her milestones right on time, even starting to walk at 10 months old! At the age of one, I noticed that she loved spinning in circles. It was the cutest thing because she would spin until she was dizzy enough to flop to the floor, and then she would laugh hysterically and try it again. Another thing I noticed about her was that she was super affectionate and attached to me, which I truly loved. That wasn't uncommon, given that she spent four weeks in the NICU away from me. So, when she was finally released to come home, she and I spent unlimited time together bonding. It wasn't the affection that got my wheels turning; it was the way she craved it, the way she desired to be squeezed with every hug, and how she wanted to hold my hand gently but also tightly at the same time.

One day, I noticed her running and hitting the walls or doors with the palms of her hands. It wasn't a gentle hit; it was very forceful each time. Initially, I thought it was out of excitement because I observed she would mostly do it during moments when something exciting happened on TV or around her. However, it eventually progressed, and she seemed to engage in this behavior throughout the day, regardless of what was happening. I began to get concerned, thinking she might eventually hurt her hand from the force she was using. So, I started redirecting her attention to other activities outside of running and hitting the doors and walls. I purchased a weighted vest, and my husband bought a trampoline to help, as I was told she was seeking pressure, which explained the forceful hitting.

The trampoline was initially acquired as an activity for all our children to enjoy indoors, but we discovered that it was particularly stimulating for our daughter. She eventually stopped running and hitting the walls and doors when she needed stimulation; instead, she began going to the trampoline to regulate herself. It was a beautiful transition to witness, realizing that something as simple as a trampoline could positively impact our daughter. There were times when I would see her holding her ears, which alarmed me every time because she was prone to ear infections. In fact, she had tubes placed in both ears due to the frequency of infections. Whenever I noticed her covering her ears, my immediate concern was that she might have another ear infection. However, I later discovered that this wasn't the case; instead, I attributed it to her molars coming in.

A doctor once explained to me that when children can't distinguish where the pain is coming from during the teething process, they might grab, tug, and hold their ears. However, I observed that this behavior had become a habit for her. At that point, I realized it wasn't solely related to her molars or an ear infection; it was my daughter revealing another unique trait about herself, which I found to be incredibly amazing. When you look at your children and see all these beautiful, unique signs, don't feel alarmed. Don't shy away, and don't feel as if you did anything wrong because you haven't. You have done everything right. In fact, you have done things perfectly, and it shows in the uniqueness of your child.

Watching my children silently express "Mommy, I'm Unique" to me wasn't easy, but I loved every moment. I found joy in every action, and I embraced who they were as my little people. I make it sound easy, right? Well, as a parent, it was easy to love them despite the reality I saw unfolding in front of me. Regardless of the reality that was beginning to set in my mind, I knew that the unique journey my children were embarking on was going to be more challenging for them than for me. I didn't have time to embrace the other emotions I was feeling. I didn't have time to space out and have a moment. My focus was to ensure that my children felt loved, understood, accepted, and confident within themselves. Although they were young and didn't quite understand many things or how they were feeling, I felt the urge to instill these things in them because eventually, they would grow to understand, and the puzzle pieces would start to come together in their little minds.

My bonus son and my daughter's unique signs showed at different times in life, but for both children, I decided to investigate resources to help them navigate through their stages; this took place without a direct diagnosis. I addressed the needs that I felt as a parent were necessary, such as speech, although there was no diagnosis stating that they had a speech delay; it was obvious to me, so I took the steps to get a speech therapist. My bonus son started with his evaluation in February of 2019. Following the evaluation, he began consistent weekly visits with the speech therapist. A few years later, February of 2022, my daughter started her speech evaluation. Following her evaluation, she also began consistent weekly visits with the speech therapist.

After taking the first steps and beginning speech therapy with my bonus son, we were told about a program called "baby net," so we investigated it, and from that point onward, my bonus son started receiving other therapies such as Occupational Therapy as well as an Early Interventionist. All of these therapies were started without a direct diagnosis of anything from his pediatrician or any other doctor. It was amazing to watch his growth. Eventually, we were asked about getting my bonus son evaluated for the spectrum, and because we were already addressing his needs and seeing progress, we agreed to the evaluation. The same applied for my daughter once it was time to address her unique needs.

The next step made us nervous but at the same time, we were as prepared as we could possibly be at that stage. We knew that no matter what results we received, nothing could change how we viewed our children and their unique and beautiful ways.

Chapter 2

The Moment of Truth "The Diagnosis"

As parents, deciding to get our child(ren) evaluated was tough because no parent wants to hear that their child may have a disability or even a delay in behavior development. As we set up the appointment, we both had to remember and come to terms with why we decided to move forward with receiving the evaluation. The evaluation wasn't being done to hinder our son and daughter; it was being done to shed light on what other steps we may need to take to help them become who they are meant to be in this world and to help us find the different tools and resources we needed as parents to ensure that our children would be successful as they grow.

The appointment process was easy. First, we took my bonus son to see his pediatrician to talk to her about the things we were noticing with him and to get her professional take on things. She confirmed that we were doing the right thing and taking the right steps. She told us that she would make a referral for him to be evaluated. She sent it on the same day to a developmental office located in Charlotte, NC, and asked that we await a phone call for further steps. Once the office received the referral from the pediatrician, they contacted my husband and me to set up a date and time for the evaluation. As we set up the appointment with the receptionist, we were informed that the evaluation was a lengthy one; it would last between 2-3 hours. They encouraged us to bring snacks and any other items that our son would need to help him feel comfortable.

The appointment day came around quickly, at least that's how it seemed to us; we were nervous going into the appointment, but we were also ready to know what was going on in our son's world. The evaluation process took about 2 hours as expected, and both my husband and I attended the appointment. When we arrived, we checked in and received forms to fill out, including a questionnaire about the concerns we had for our son. Once we completed the forms, we were escorted to the back and into the waiting area.

When it was time for the testing only one parent was allowed in the room, so I decided to sit with our youngest son at the time and allow my husband to accompany my bonus son during his testing because I felt that he needed to be present in the room. My husband struggled with the experience more than I did.

I saw the hurt in his eyes when we were informed about getting my bonus son evaluated, I saw the worry in him, and I felt that if he was present in the room to see what would take place in the evaluation he could possibly be more at ease with the process. After the first hour, I was allowed to accompany both my husband and bonus son into the room to discuss what took place. I was very intrigued as the evaluator explained to me the variety of tasks that they did with my bonus son and how everything was done through play. Then they informed us that they would be stepping out to score the parental questionnaire as well as the things they saw during the evaluation. As my husband and I waited patiently, we sat and talked amongst ourselves and watched our two boys play.

We had been sitting anxiously when the evaluators returned, and we knew that it was time for the moment of truth. We were informed that the scoring indicated that our son was on the spectrum. They told us that there are three levels of ASD (Autism Spectrum Disorder), and our son was diagnosed with level two which means that he required substantial support. A level two child is a child who has marked difficulties in verbal and nonverbal social communication skills, they typically have restricted repetitive behavior, and noticeable difficulties changing activities or focusing. However, the good news was that we were already receiving services and going in the right direction. We were told about another therapy which they call ABA therapy, which stands for Applied Behavior Analysis. This therapy is typically considered for children who have Autism or other developmental disorders. We received a list of places that had an open waitlist for ABA therapy, a handout about genetics testing, community places that held events for families with children who were on the spectrum, a list of support groups, and more. The evaluator told us we were already on the right track and doing amazingly. It was a substantial amount of information to process, but as soon as we made it home, I began to read through all the paperwork we received.

Immediately, I called to set up the genetic testing for my husband and bonus son. I contacted my bonus son's biological mother to inform her that she would need to be present for genetic testing on behalf of our son. I began putting my bonus son on the ABA therapies waitlist and researching ASD because I had no common knowledge about what it was, what to expect, or how to properly care for a child with Autism. I did find some helpful tools, but the majority of my tools came from day-to-day experience with him because there were so many things he did that I couldn't find help for from my research. There were even moments when his therapists couldn't give me answers because his unique ways were new to them as well. I remember nights where he would sit up in the middle of his bed like a zombie while still asleep, or he would get out of bed and be standing next to our bed while still asleep. It scared me because I feared that he would eventually start sleepwalking. My husband worked the night shift, so my bonus son was always with me during the night. I spoke to my husband about it and recommended that we take him to the doctor to see what steps we could take to help our son with what he was experiencing at night. I didn't know what to call it and to this day I still don't know what to call it. The pediatrician referred us to a specialist to make sure he wasn't having seizures at night or night terrors. We received a call from the receptionist at Piedmont Hospital to set up an overnight stay for our son. We set up the appointment and I began praying that everything would come back okay with him. At the same time, my husband and I started preparing ourselves for another diagnosis, especially considering the fact that my husband suffered from fibroid seizures up until he was 5 years old.

My husband and I both attended the overnight stay. We watched as they hooked our son up to monitors and wrapped bands around him to prevent him from snatching off any cords. He did well with being hooked up; he laughed, watched TV, ate snacks, and eventually once he fell asleep, they began monitoring his brain. We were discharged to go home the next morning. The doctors advised us that they would contact us to go over the results after they had reviewed them. It took about a week before we heard anything from the nurse. Finally, she called and informed us that everything came back in good standing; they didn't see any evidence of seizures on his brain. That was some of the best news we could receive, we were so grateful. We were told that there wasn't a way to tell if he was having night terrors or not, but they wanted to follow up with him within 6 months to ensure nothing had progressed or changed. We scheduled the 6-month follow-up appointment and continued to monitor him through the night.

Eventually, the behavior stopped. I don't know what caused it to happen or what caused it to stop, but I was thankful that it was no longer happening because it was a terrifying feeling, and I was losing so much sleep from the fear that he may sleepwalk. The next step we were to take was genetic testing. Since COVID was on the rise, we were unable to go into the office to do testing. Instead, Greenville Genetics Testing Center sent the kits to our home and my bonus son's biological Mom. My husband had to swab his mouth as well as our son's mouth and his biological Mom had to swab her mouth as well. Once completed, the kits were to be sent back to the genetics center for testing. We completed a phone interview in June of 2020, consenting to the testing. In July 2020 we received the kits, completed them, and sent them back in.

It took a few months, but we finally received the results back and were able to conduct another phone interview to go over the findings. Many of the results were inconclusive, which means they didn't find anything in the Mom's or the Dad's genetics that would result in my bonus son being diagnosed with his uniqueness. This also means we may never know what led to the diagnosis. One thing I do know is our son and daughter were both diagnosed with ASD. Although we are pending the genetic testing of our daughter, I am certain that we may never know what caused her diagnosis either. I am okay with that because I believe in my heart that God created them to be different for a purpose. They are unique for a reason and whatever that reason is, I embrace it as much as I possibly can.

I took our daughter in for evaluation in October of 2022. During this time, we knew what to expect with the evaluation because of what we experienced with our son. Our daughter's evaluation was a little different because we were now staying in a different city, but the same state. Her pediatrician referred her to a place called Developmental Peds. They had a waitlist for her age bracket that ranged between 3-6 months from the referral date. We waited and waited, then we finally received the call to get her in for testing. First, we had to conduct a telehealth appointment, which lasted about an hour. A week later we were able to get the evaluation appointment. She was able to get an appointment quickly because the office had a cancellation. My husband and I were now parents of three toddlers so, he stayed home with our oldest two boys, while I took our daughter to the appointment.

This time, I was able to witness firsthand how the evaluation was conducted and how they calculated the score. There were two evaluators in the room. I answered a series of questions with one, while the other one interacted, played with, and evaluated our daughter. I watched in amazement because as I previously stated about my bonus son's evaluation, it was interesting to see that they could assess through play. The appointment lasted 2 hours, as it did with my bonus son. Once complete, the evaluators left to score the parental assessment along with their findings. It took them about 30-35 minutes before they returned with the results. I was informed that their findings, along with the information I provided, indicated that our daughter was on the spectrum. She too was considered to be level two on the spectrum. They provided me with pamphlets just as we were provided for my bonus son. These pamphlets were for the current city we stayed in.

As I did for my bonus son, I went straight home and started putting her on waiting lists for ABA therapy and setting up genetic testing for her. I didn't have much to get in place for her because we had already been in therapy for 8 months. Our daughter's signs were much different from our son's signs; I wouldn't have guessed she was on the spectrum. In fact, my husband and I were sure that her being nonverbal was due to her being a premature baby. The only similarity she shared with her big brother was that they both were nonverbal. We learned that all children on the spectrum are different; they all have different ways of showing that they are unique- that's what makes them so special, their individuality is like no other. My daughter didn't struggle with half the things our son struggled with, yet they both were diagnosed with level two ASD. Amazing right? Our daughter started walking on her tiptoes so often that I decided to seek an evaluation from a physical therapist.

My husband thought I was overreacting, he insisted that nothing was wrong with her feet. As mothers, we tend to have an undeniable intuition that sometimes fathers may not understand; it's that special little gift God placed on the inside of us. It's why we are considered to be the nurturers of our babies. Does it mean a father's role or instinct is less important or valid? Absolutely not! However, sometimes, fathers struggle with the reality of things when it comes to their child(ren) even if they can visibly see it. I decided to reach out to her early interventionist to set up an evaluation for physical therapy, just to ensure nothing was wrong with her legs or feet. Being a preemie, there's a possibility of issues arising as she grows.

I finally received a call from a physical therapist in reference to coming out for an evaluation. It was an in-home appointment which made it convenient. The therapist came out to see our baby girl; it was a simple evaluation. He asked me a series of questions, exercised her legs and feet then watched her walk for a little while so that he could witness the tiptoe walking, which she did as he was observing her. She never consistently stayed on her toes, it was always on and off. I was informed that right now, since she was walking on them less than 50% of the time there was no need for physical therapy. I was also advised to monitor it. If she began walking on them more than 50% of the time, she would need physical therapy and possibly braces to wear inside her shoes to help regulate the tiptoe walking. The therapist told me that because she is a child who seeks sensory pressure, she was possibly walking on her tiptoes on and off like that to stimulate herself, which made perfect sense to me. I was thankful that there wasn't another diagnosis or a need for another therapy.

Receiving a diagnosis can be hard but we must understand that a diagnosis does not define who we are as people, it's merely the identification of the nature of an illness or other problem through examination of the symptoms. We can't allow the fear of receiving a diagnosis to keep us from getting to the bottom of what our child is dealing with. I know in this day and age, many parents are fearful of what others may think, how others may view their child(ren), or what could be said. As a mother and bonus mother of children who received a diagnosis, I am here to tell you to block out the noise of naysayers, ignore the thoughts of others, and forget how others may view you or your child. Step up and step out on behalf of your child(ren). Don't allow their need to go unnoticed; you are their voice. If you don't stand up for them and get them the help that they need they will become another statistic in society. Trust me when I tell you, it's not worth the gamble.

Chapter 3

Accepting My Au-someness

Finding out that your child is on the spectrum can be hard to hear and it can also be hard to accept, especially when we don't know why it's happening to our little ones or what caused the diagnosis. Nothing or no one can prepare us for a journey like this. It's impossible not to go blind as you're facing the reality of the diagnosis, especially when you have little to no experience with handling a child on the spectrum. Yes, at the onset it can be quite overwhelming and very heart breaking. The diagnosis may seem like bad news, but hang in there, it's not! We often get stuck on the term "disability" because in our minds it means disabled which means unable to do certain things or limited with certain things, but I want to open your minds to a brighter side of a spectrum diagnosis, I want to give you a positive outlook about children on the spectrum.

Let's not focus on the word disability, let's not get it stuck in our heads that our children are limited to the things they can do or that our children will be unable to do the things that a child who is not on the spectrum can do. I know from experience that is not true. When my husband and I got the diagnosis for our son we had many questions and concerns, as any parent who has just received news about their child being on the spectrum would have. We wondered if he would be able to care for himself as he got older, if he would have any type of independence, would he function in public places, and if he would be capable of making friends. Our biggest concerns were whether he would ever say words and how he would communicate with us and others. Trust me when I say I know what you are feeling after receiving the diagnosis. Also trust me when I say your child has autism; autism does not have your child. That means your child is in control of the diagnosis, not the other way around. Your child is resilient, smart, strong, and very capable of being anything he or she desires to be in this world, just as much as a child who isn't on the spectrum.

Do you know why? Well, let me tell you! It's because your child is AU-SOME! The definition of Au-some is similar to the word "awesome" but it's a bit more special, just like your child(ren)! Each letter symbolizes a beautiful characteristic of your child:

A is for Amazing

U is for Unique

S is for Smart

O is for Optimistic

M is for Magical

E is for Empowered

That alone says so much about our little ones on the spectrum, I no longer look at my children and wonder what they are or will be capable of when I look at them. I see so many possibilities; a full and bright future and unlimited stars that they can reach because the sky isn't the limit for them. They will soar above and beyond the expectations of those around them. The moment we started to accept our son's Au-someness, we started to see beautiful things happen ten-fold for him. The questions that we had at the beginning of this journey were no longer there. My bonus son showed us his true colors from the start, and he continued to show us how bright he could be day by day. Although we are still at the beginning of our daughter's Au-some journey, we don't question anything with her because we have seen from experience how things can turn around for the greater good. Even if her story turns out to be different from the story of our son's, we won't waver because we know that she still has a story to tell - just in her own way. We accept her Au-someness in whatever form it shows up in.

Accepting that your child is Au-some does not mean you have to let go of the dreams you had for them, it doesn't mean you have to let go of the expectations you had for them from the moment you found out about their existence, it just means you have to alter those dreams and expectations to fit the Au-some needs of your child(ren). Your child can still become the doctor you dreamed they would be, they can still become a lawyer. Their dreams, nor your dream for them is impossible. Though it may be delayed, it's not denied, it will happen for them just at their pace and that is perfectly fine. It will not do you or your child any good to become bitter about their reality, you may not know it but these unique and Au-some little people can feel things far beyond our belief, when our emotions change, they can feel it, when our tone changes, they can feel it. They may be unable to tell us what they are feeling or how they noticed a shift in our emotions but trust me they do.

As their parents, you don't want them to feel anything less than supported and most importantly accepted by you and those around them. In order for others to weigh in on accepting our brilliant child(ren) we have to first lead by example because it starts at home with us. Accepting your reality and who your child is in this stage of life will open so many doors and avenues for both you and your child(ren). Acceptance gives room for growth and that is something we desire to see consistently on this journey. Whether that growth comes through communication or the things your child has learned to do physically or emotionally that they were unable to do before, all growth is good. Growth comes in many different forms and every little accomplishment is major for our babies, nothing should go unnoticed because each new thing learned is a step forward in the right direction.

Remember to always have an open mind because on this journey anything is possible. Here are a few ways you can learn to accept your child's Au-someness, it helped me, so I want to pass it on as a tool to help all my amazing and Au-some Moms and Dads. The first step is to acknowledge your feelings. That means noticing how you feel as things happen and writing those feelings down. Next, allow yourself to feel those feelings in the rawest form. Take the time you need to cry and release the pain in your personal time. Whether that be in the shower, in your room at night, or even in your car; you need to let it out. Be sure while allowing yourself to be vulnerable, also be kind to yourself, and don't beat yourself up about how you feel because your feelings are valid. You aren't wrong for having a moment. You needed that moment to continue to press on and move forward. You needed that moment to give you strength. You needed that moment to release and let go of what was so that you can focus on what is. Your next step would be to create a strong support system. Just as you are the support for your child, you need someone to hold you up in your moments of weakness.

Lastly, make sure you pray. Ask God to help you not lean on your own understanding but to trust the journey he has blessed you to take. Prayer can take you a long way and if you are a believer in Christ, you know if He brings you to it, He will bring you through it each and every time. God will never bring you this far on your journey to leave you. Even when you can't feel him, He is there by your side walking hand and hand with you guiding you through all the obstacles and stumbling blocks. My bonus son was nonverbal for the first 2 ½ years of his life, he didn't so much as babble when we started this journey with him. We were so discouraged doing therapy after therapy. It seemed like no progress was being made. Working with him outside of therapy and seeing again what looked to us like no progress was discouraging, but we stayed consistent and faithful. Here we are now with a five-year-old toddler who has exceeded our expectations. The progress he has made speaks for itself. He went from being a nonverbal child to verbal, he knows and recognizes his ABCs, numbers, and shapes. He can tell you his full name, birthday, age, the names of all 4 of his siblings, all 3 parents, and is now learning to read. His teacher says he is at the top of his kindergarten class, academically. We may have hiccups or bumps along the way but that is to be expected. I said all of that to say: acceptance is key. My husband and I are so proud of where our son is today, we look back at where we started from and rejoice because we didn't think we would be where we are today.

Yes, we lost hope a few times, and we struggled with acceptance, but we fought through it all, humbled ourselves, and allowed our son to lead the way. I want to encourage my Au-some parents of nonverbal children as well because every story has a different ending. If your ending wasn't your child going from nonverbal to verbal know and understand that your child is just as Au-some as those that went from nonverbal to verbal. What I love about children that are nonverbal is their ability to communicate using their bodies. Not many people can do that, but your child(ren) can, and I consider that to be beautiful. A nonverbal child can teach us so many things. I am currently learning that with my daughter, who is currently nonverbal, the way she communicates with me is so different and challenging at times, but the outcome is so amazing.

One thing my daughter has taught me about being nonverbal is that I must listen to her with more than just my ears. I absolutely enjoy learning new ways to listen to and understand her. If you are the parent to a nonverbal child, I want you to continue to journey with faith and know that your child isn't less than others; they are greater than. They are greater than their circumstance, greater than the statistics, greater than the diagnosis, greater than the expectations that are constantly placed on them, and greater than the words they cannot verbally say. Your child is speaking to you through their personality, through sign language, through body gestures, and through their pure little hearts. So, do your best to open yourself up to their world. Many times, the answer is in watching our child(ren) in the moment. It's hard to hear your child through unacceptance, it's hard to understand them through unacceptance. I know this because I was that parent, I put on a brave face around other people but in the back of my mind, I wasn't in a place to accept my children's Au-someness because it would have made their diagnosis surreal. Here I am now, in a place of acceptance watching my daughter grow.

Although she's unable to talk to me verbally, I am learning so much just by watching. I am able to understand her moments and I am able to hear her even when she's not saying much. I know what every grunt means, I know what her high-pitched tone means, and I know when she is feeling excited and overwhelmed just by the sounds she's making. I know when she is ready for a nap just by the slight little whine she lets out and that for me is an amazing place to be in. It's a beautiful feeling hearing my child through her silent moments. I don't believe she will be nonverbal forever and I don't believe your child(ren) will be nonverbal forever, I just think they haven't figured out how to unlock their superpower yet.

Once they do, you will see a change so great in them that it's going to blow your mind. I encourage you to hang in there, buckle in, and hold on to your seat because you are about to go on the ride of your life, and your child is the driver. Trust me, you're going to enjoy every moment of it. So, relax on the passenger side, look around and sightsee on this journey, and embrace all the colors that you see along the way, all while you mentally capture pictures along the way. Once you arrive at your destination, take a moment to bask in how far you and your child(ren) have come, reflect on the journey you have had thus far, but don't stay there too long. There is more to see, there are other avenues and cities to travel to as well. The road has not yet come to an end, this is just a pit stop so that you can gas up and travel further. You are now on your way to helping your child(ren) find the key to unlock their superpowers.

Chapter 4

Unlocking My Superpower

For every lock there is a key, you can't go into your home without unlocking the door and you can't get into your vehicle without unlocking the door first, right? Right! Well, that is the same method to use for your child(ren)'s superpower. We can't access who they truly are without unlocking their minds; they are so full of thoughts, ideas, and even words but they can't express them because they haven't tapped into their capabilities. They are unsure of the things they know. They are also unsure of the things they feel and can say. However, every superhero has a sidekick and for your child, you are that sidekick. A sidekick is a person's assistant or close associate. They typically have less authority than the superhero, which in this case is completely okay because our job as their sidekick is to help them learn what their capabilities are on their journey so that we can send them out into the world equipped to take on any and everything that is designed to hinder them. Once they learn what they are capable of they are a step closer to finding the key to unlocking their superpowers and we are a step closer to having successful and unstoppable children.

We talked about steps one and two of unlocking their superpower in chapter three. Yes, ACCEPTANCE and EMBRACING are the first two steps to finding the key, the next step would be accountability. What that means is you have to hold yourself accountable for the things your child learns and picks up while on this mission. You have to be accountable for getting them to that key because they are unable to do it alone. Which is why they have Au-some sidekicks for parents. We can do anything we put our minds to and that is what we show along the way, when we lose our way, we must remember to look at our map and get back on track. The map that we are using isn't just any old map. Our map, just like everything else on this mission - is unique. It consists of our support team, the teachers, and the therapist that were put in place to guide us through. They will give us the directions, step by step. While our children depend on us to help unlock their superpowers, we are depending on the educational team to lead us to the keys because they have all the information and tools that we need to help them. There is no better road map to utilize than that. The third and final step is to simply follow through. This step is the most crucial and sometimes most difficult because this step requires action and sometimes action isn't as easy as it sounds. It takes an extensive amount of drive and work, but don't worry, you're not acting alone. You have your superhero right by your side fighting too, and there is no duo like parent and child. They are the strength of the operation, and we are the voice. I enjoyed being the voice of my bonus son while we worked towards unlocking his superpower.

Watching him work so hard to accomplish goals that were set in place by the therapist gave me the strength to work harder. He wanted to learn new things and he was excited about each therapy. Even the carryover we did at home kept him intrigued. I saw how intrigued and eager he was to unlock those powers that lie beneath the surface of his mind. Because of that, each day we would do something of substance, things that would challenge his mind. I could literally see the wheels turning. I watched how he thought and solved problems. I knew we were getting closer to finding out what superpowers he carried. One day, out of the blue, my bonus son started saying letters while we watched TV. I didn't pay it any attention because he loved to say ABCs.

Although he wasn't saying them in order, I figured he just enjoyed saying letters until I realized he was pointing to letters on my t-shirt and saying them. I was completely in shock, so I decided to get up and grab something else with letters on it, and sure enough, he read each letter. That's when I knew not only did he know the alphabet but he could also recognize them anywhere. It blew me out of the water because I had never worked on letter recognition with him. I immediately started to praise him and tell him how proud I was that he could now recognize his letters.

Then a lightbulb went off in my head and I instantly knew what his superpower was! We finally found the key that unlocks all understanding and unlocks the powers we knew were there all along. Our son's superpower is the way he thinks, obtains information, and remembers it. Even though I didn't work on letter recognition with him, he figured out how to recognize the letters simply by doing the alphabet when we would work on putting together the alphabet puzzle. It never dawned on me that he was silently picking up what each letter looked like because my focus was solely on getting him accustomed to knowing his ABCs. He's an intelligent child and once we unlocked his superpower he only got better. Everything we taught him, he picked up quickly and it would stick with him. But like any other new superhero, he had to learn what to do with his newfound superpower. We knew what it was but he didn't quite understand how to use it or when to use it so he would go to school and the teachers would think he didn't know certain things. They would contact me letting me know what he needed to work on and the things they listed would always surprise me because he was already doing them really well at home; the same applied to therapy.

I started talking with him about showing his teachers and therapists his amazing work, so that they could also see his capabilities and understand his superpower, but he would still go to school and therapy and pretend he didn't know or couldn't do certain things. My next step was to show his teachers and therapists through video so I began recording when we would work on certain things. I started sending it to the teachers and therapists and they were completely in awe because they were under the impression that he couldn't do it. Once he knew that I informed those around him about his superpowers we began to see him progress in school and therapy. He was now comfortable showing off his powers. Realizing what you are capable of can be a bit scary sometimes, especially for our unique children. Even as adults, we get overwhelmed with knowing our capabilities, so imagine how your little one may feel after unlocking such a big part of who they are.

Unlocking their superpower is a big step to take, but after we find the key and unlock who they truly are, we also must help them learn what it means to be powerful and what it means to be unique. Ultimately, we must help them learn what it means to be a superhero. We must teach them that it's okay to show off their powers because the world needs to see it. Reassure them that they have these powers for a reason and that reason is so they can one day help someone just like them. Our son is only in kindergarten, but he loves teaching, even at home with his siblings. He is always using his superpower to help his brother and sister. When his brother is learning and he gets stuck on something, he swoops in with his cape on to save the day to help guide his brother to the answer. Even in school, his teacher tells us how he helps his friends in the classroom. It took a while, but he is now in full control of his superpowers, he knows when to use them and how to use them appropriately. We have our own personal hero who loves his superpower and is confident in it.

We are now on the journey of finding out our daughter's superpower. I know it is within her waiting to scratch the surface as well. My husband and I like to say that her powers are shy at this stage, but eventually, they will come full circle and she will be ready to take on the world, one task at a time, right next to her Au-some big brother. There isn't a timeframe for figuring out what superpower your child(ren) carries. Much like many other things, it takes time. You will know when it's time to unlock those powers, your child will show signs of readiness. There are typically five characteristics of becoming a superhero and I think, better yet I know, your child(ren) carries all of those traits. Super strength is one of those traits and we have already established that our children exemplify strength. I consider that strength to be both physical and mental. Superintelligence is another trait our children excel in. Children who are uniquely on the spectrum are some of the smartest children I know, and their intelligence is one of a kind. It's truly amazing watching how they solve problems on a day-to-day basis. Our superheroes have the trait of being courageous; they are such brave little people. The outstanding part about it is that they have no clue how brave they are; they are doing it effortlessly. They are also very inspirational. Yes, another characteristic I see and admire about our superheroes is how inspirational they are to us as their parents and to those around them. They naturally inspire others in so many ways. I can't tell you how inspired I have been since becoming an Au-some parent.

My children have brought me out of so many dark places just by being joyous and simply being themselves. Last, but certainly not least, they have determination. As a mother, this trait is so magnificent to see in them, because I've never seen such little people be in a place of determination. Unknowingly, they genuinely give everything they do their all, even through the frustrating moments of stubbornness or not understanding what they are doing, they give it the best they have because they are determined to master a task. They take the saying "Giving up is not an option" to a whole new level. Typically, their focus is off but when you are watching them fight to focus, you are looking at determination in its purest form. When you watch them struggle to complete a task and you see the frustration kick in, yet they still work to continue and finish that task, that is determination at its best. Determination is firmness of purpose. Although our babies may not know what their purpose is, they are standing firm in it; it's unbelievable yet incredible to watch. When you look at your child(ren) you are going to see all these things I described within them. These characteristics among so many others make your superhero powerful. I see these characteristics in my daughter, and that's how I know one day she will make a beautiful superhero. Right now, we are at a point where she hasn't shown signs of being ready to reveal her powers. She is still in the beginning stages of finding her way, so until she is ready, I will continue to fight her battles for her because that's my job as her sidekick. She holds the key to her own success and superpowers. I am just patiently waiting to travel through her Au-some little mind to find what she is fantastic at.

Your child will show signs of readiness to let you know it's time to search for the key that unlocks their powers and the signs will be crystal clear to you. It's something like intuition, you will feel it just as you will see it. You will automatically know just as I did with my bonus son. All children's readiness signs are different so there is nothing specific you should look for. As a parent, you know your child, even in the moments when you feel as if you know nothing about them, you do! They are going to evolve into greatness, so beware and keep a watchful eye and before you know it you will be on the journey of raising a captivating, graceful, ambitious, and impressive superhero. There is more to your child than meets the eye.

Chapter 5

The Journey

Taking a journey is an act of traveling from one place to another. Albeit, being on a journey doesn't always mean physical travel. Sometimes our journey is the things we are taking on in life, a transition from one phase in life to the next. Autism is a journey because we are always traveling through phases. These phases are like adventures, except there is no real danger at hand; only excitement. We are the adventurers because we seek success for our child(ren) while on this journey. We wear the hats of many job titles just like our children, but these hats are needed in each area. They are what make the journey worthwhile and fulfilling. I would like to touch base on each phase that we have to encounter on this journey and the importance of being steadfast and purposeful while going through the transitions.

There are several phases that we will have to transition into and transition out of as we travel. We must remember the importance of transitioning; it's just a part of life. No matter what happens in life, we must evolve and change because staying in one phase for too long can hinder us from the possibilities that await us. Every transition has a three-phase process: an ending, a neutral zone, and a new beginning. We are going to start by tackling phase one of the transition process, the ending stage. You may be thinking about how we can start transitioning with an ending, but I want to reassure you that all transitions start with an ending because you will have to end something before starting something new.

For example, before you can start a new relationship, first you have to be done with the previous relationship you had. Much like before you can start reading a new book you first have to end the last chapter of the previous book. The same applies here, you can't begin a new phase on this journey without completing or ending the phase you are currently in, or else it will throw everything off balance and cause quite a bit of confusion for your child(ren). Being that they are already having trouble finding their way along this journey, this is the last thing we want to do.

First, you need to attempt to understand all aspects of the phase you are currently in. Then you need to visualize the changes that will start to take place one at a time; figure out what losses you may have to endure and accept them as they come. Sometimes in life, the things we may see as a loss aren't really a loss; it's a gain. Many times, we get so caught up in the pain of letting go that we can't see what we will be gaining by moving forward from the things we desire. There is no harm in reacting to the things you are leaving behind. I mean, after all, we are learning to transition, so emotional reactions are expected to happen along the way. Don't stay in that emotional or reaction state too long because we now have to seek out understanding. We must now understand that certain things will happen, especially things out of our control. That's when we must accept the things we cannot change while working on the things we can change; this stage is very vital. Always keep an open mind and communicate.

Now that we know all about how to phase into and out of the ending stage let's move on to the neutral zone. This phase can be tricky because this is where you will realize there is no going back, you can only move forward. Looking back will distract you. Notice how in the movies when someone is being chased, as they run and look forward, they are getting away rather smoothly, but the moment they start to look back to see what is behind them they begin to stumble, fall, and trip over things? Well, that is exactly what will happen if you start looking back after entering this stage. You will begin to lose your balance and the things you have left behind or transitioned out of will start to catch up with you. We don't want that on the journey with us, do we? Absolutely not!

This journey is all about moving forward, it's solely about gain. While we are in the neutral zone, we should strive to keep the demands we place on ourselves reasonable. Our expectations of things cannot be high, and this is when we begin to set short-term and long-term goals. These goals must be realistic for the parents as well as our children. Remember, this journey is not just about us, it's about our sweet babies as well. We want them to be able to accomplish the goals we set forth for them. Don't rush through this phase, give yourself and your child(ren) time to explore the things to come because there will be so many things happening in this stage that you both will be unfamiliar with. The key is to allow it to happen; ask the necessary questions, give your honest concerns, and ask for directions when needed. This goes hand in hand with communication. One thing you will learn through each phase is that you will have to have strong communication. You will need to have a voice because without it you won't get very far.

We are now making progress on this journey. We are ready to transition from the neutral stage, which is so uncomfortable, and transition into a more comfortable stage. A happy stage, the phase we have all been waiting for. This stage is the new beginning. This phase is like a breath of fresh air, it's equivalent to that first cup of coffee to get your day started each morning. It's needed just as breakfast is needed during the morning because as they say breakfast is the most important meal of the day. Well, the new beginning is the most important stage of the journey. New beginnings tend to give us mixed emotions.

We first feel fear or nervousness because this is new and although it's everything I just described, it's also the not knowing what's to come part that can and will set in on us unexpectedly. When you are purposeful, change feels so much more tolerable. When you can see the future clearly, the fear fades and turns into excitement because now you know what to expect and you are in a place of rejoicing for better things and better days. When you are a part of the transition with a real and authentic role to play on this journey with your child(ren) when you aren't feeling like an outcast or a helpless participant in your child's journey, you are able to exemplify excitement and you're able to see the beauty in the journey. Stay consistent with those long-term and short-term goals you set in the last phase, or you'll lose sight of where you're headed. Grab hold of your support system so they can encourage you along the way. Start a narrative about your new. Start with enthusiasm and positive intent and don't forget to celebrate. Celebrate a fresh start for both you and your child(ren). Be sure to celebrate the new beginning, and always take one step at a time, there is no need to rush.

Being steadfast means being unwavering on this journey. You will see a plethora of things come in to test your ability to stand firm and be unwavering, but you must stick with your beliefs on this journey because you must do what is best and what works for both of you. The Bible says Christ creates and blesses a steadfast heart, so we need to have steadfast faith to keep us in pursuit of the Lord even when life gets difficult. Do you know why? Because in light of all things you have to keep the fire burning. What I mean by that is you have to keep going despite anything; you have to remain determined, and you must keep that drive about yourself because those three things will ensure that you don't lose hope or get lost on this journey. You must be diligent. When you do something diligently, you put your entire heart into it. You don't give up; you give it all you got; in doing so you will be rewarded. The Greek definition of "reward" means one who pays wages, that alone puts things in a new perspective.

We will earn our wages(reward) of discovering more on this journey when we put the work in by diligently seeking things out as we go. On this journey, I encourage you to ask God for grace to continue, and never be satisfied or complacent with completing a phase. I say that because there is always more to be accomplished and more to be discovered about your child. I stated this before and I will state it again, the journey does not end here.

Let's talk about being purposeful on our journey. Mom and Dad, if someone is purposeful it means they are showing that they have a definite aim and a strong desire to achieve it. Going to college, starting a family, giving to charity, adopting a pet, etc. are some things we purposely do, those are purposeful acts. Personally speaking, I have had a few purposeful acts on this journey with my two children, I became a stay-at-home Mom who works as a CNA as needed, which we typically call PRN. I create my own schedule by signing up for days that I have free. That was a purposeful act for me because I aimed to get my children what they needed in each and every aspect possible. In doing so I felt I needed to be as physically present as possible. I had a strong desire to see them win, to see them be great, to see them gain success, to see them meet milestones, and to see them grow into amazing, selfless, and confident humans. That is still my desire because our journey has not ended.

Although my bonus son is a few years into his journey, he still has so much more to gain and to learn and we are just now getting started on our daughter's journey. So, Moms and Dads, I urge you to be purposeful with everything you do on your journey with your child; do whatever it takes. Your journey doesn't have to be what mine is, your aim can be so much more, and it can be different. I want you to find your aim and strongly desire it. You do this by developing purposeful thinking. Allow me to elaborate a little more on what that requires and means. Purposeful thinking is clear, certain, and efficient. To develop that mindset, you need to know there is no wasted energy on negative things. There is no need to overcompensate positive thinking, no need for pleasure-seeking distractions. We are truly aligned with our purpose when we are thinking purposefully and being purposeful; we can feel it. This journey is going to take you through some things, meaning, it's not going to be rainbows and clear skies all the time. It's not going to be sunny days every single day with no rain. When you hold on to being purposeful, you hold on to being steadfast and you hold on to being intentional.

While all of that is true, believe me when I tell you, there won't be a storm that you can't weather. I've fought through some storms on our journey and every now and then I still must grab my raincoat, rainboots, and umbrella to gear up for another stormy day. I refuse to lose sight of the goals I have when those moments arise. I don't forget what my aim is for my children, and I think that's the part that keeps me hanging on in our everyday life. I may go through these changes and face the rain but one thing I'm never going to allow to happen on our journey is allow my children to get wet from the storms we face. They don't know the things we are going through to make it through this journey with them and they should never know because they are our blessings. They didn't choose this journey; the journey chose them.

Alongside my husband, we are proud to have such Au-some children to travel with. I couldn't imagine a better tour guide than the ones I have by my side, my

Tinkerbell, and my Macho Man. These nicknames for our babies originated when they were infants but now that I know how unique and Au-some they are. I feel that these names were destined to be. My daughter is Tinker Bell because she is so magical and beautiful. She is very sassy, feisty, and sometimes stubborn, all of which makes her who she is; I love it. My bonus son is my Macho Man because he has always had such confidence in himself; he's always exemplified strength, honor, bravery, and nobleness and I've always adored that about him. While we have come a mighty long way, I want to end this chapter by saying THE JOURNEY CONTINUES.

Chapter 6

Change Is Inevitable

When it comes to change, our Au-some child(ren) aren't a major fan of it. Change can be scary for them, and it can cause friction within them. It's almost like shaking up a soda bottle and then opening it up. What typically happens in that scenario is that the soda explodes everywhere. That's exactly what takes place when you aren't consistent with your child(ren)'s routines or when you create regular changes with your child(ren). When change occurs, especially unexpectedly, it causes your child to respond negatively. All children respond differently, but most of our Au-some children respond by tantrums, repetitive behaviors, aggression, and even withdrawal. It is extremely important to remember that your child is exhibiting these things because they can't communicate their feelings or emotions the right way. Changes happen daily, it's a part of life. As an Au-some Mom of two, I understand that all changes can't be prevented. This means at some point, a meltdown is bound to happen. Along this journey, I have also learned that we must do our best to prepare them for the changes to come, especially if we are aware of the change before it must happen.

One way I prepare my children for changes, major or minor, is through short stories. I often create personal short stories for them, I make them realistic and relatable for my children. I have found them to be super successful with my little ones. I read the short story to them daily, all the way up until the change happens. That way they can smoothly transition into a new era or phase. I learned that our little superheroes don't like surprises; they like to know what's going to happen and when. That's not uncommon at all, I mean I too like to know things before they happen. The difference is I can handle changes without knowing and my children can't.

Another method I used and found to be helpful is the "first and then" method; my bonus son's teacher taught me this method. It was used for him in his first year of school to help him transition and I utilized that method at home; it worked wonders. I was able to get him to do most of his day-to-day activities by using this method. Even now at age 5, he uses it completely on his own when he is trying to remember to complete tasks at home and it is still helpful in school as well. Also, everything must be visible for your child(ren). Yes, visuals are important, especially in the early stages, when they are young because they get to see what they are doing. As they get older, they may or may not need the visuals, it just depends on your child and how they operate with transitions. My bonus son still requires visuals because without them he is unsettled.

Using a calendar is a personal method I chose to use to help my bonus son with transitions. I used stickers to color code his calendar, then I taught him the meaning of each color so when he saw a specific color, he knew it was either therapy day, school, weekend time with his biological Mom, doctor appointment day, etc. He always knew what to expect just by seeing a certain color on his calendar for the day at hand. We still utilize the calendar method because he is accustomed to it, and he enjoys seeing what's to come next. I also utilized a visual timer, an idea I received from my bonus son's teacher. We visited her class one day, and I noticed it in the class; I asked his teacher about it, and I asked how she normally utilizes it. She gave me pointers for when to use it. The timer was being used for transitions. I was so intrigued when I returned home so I began my internet search. Of course, I found it on Amazon, because of course... Amazon has everything!

I began using it at home to get my bonus son to transition from one activity to the next such as playing with toys and then putting them away. I found it to be amazing! The timer worked miracles in our household, even with our middle son who has a speech impairment and social/emotional delay. Our middle son would struggle with transitions just as much as our oldest son, so I incorporated the timer with both of them and surely before I knew it, they were learning to transition with ease because of the timer. To this day, both of our sons will ask how many minutes they must do certain tasks, or they look for the timer when they are doing tasks around the house. It's truly amazing! These are just a few personal routes I chose to take with my children that I found to be a great help in making changes easy for them.

My bonus son struggled with changes more than my daughter. Right now, it is easy for our daughter to transition from one task to another. As she gets older, it's possible that it will change, so I still use these methods with her to make it routine, just in case things change as she grows older. I love taking preventative measures and although a lot of things that worked for our son may not work for our daughter, I feel it is worth a shot. If it fails, I can find what works for her and utilize it. I encourage you to practice doing new activities with your child(ren), use some of these methods, or come up with your own methods that you feel can help your child with change. Apply them and watch how your child learns to handle change in the best way possible and watch how they learn to transition. If your child is preparing for school, please attend the meet and greet and bring your child so they can meet the person they will see for the remainder of the year.

After the meet and greet, create visuals about school that will help them transition when the first day comes around. When they have appointments coming up, talk to them about the doctor, and allow them to know where they are going and why they have to go ahead of time. It takes an extensive amount of time and energy to help them transition in their everyday life, but it will make going places and leaving places so much easier and less of a hassle if they simply know what to expect. Allow your child time to adjust to changes and provide them with a role in the transition that's taking place. For example, if you are ready to put away the puzzle and start Mr. Potato Head, but your child(ren) is having a hard time changing activities, they are just in a place of refusal when it comes to transition. At that moment you can simply ask them to help you clean, help you find Mr. Potato Head, etc. That's giving them a role that helps incorporate them in the change. It can also help them want to do more or want to move on to something new. It's always exciting to help; kids love to do so.

When I first had my middle son, my bonus son was about to turn 1 years old, so he didn't quite understand the importance of having a role or helping out. He and his younger brother really grew together but when I had my daughter, my bonus son was age 3 and my middle son was age 2, so they were older, and they both understood that they would soon have a baby sister.

My bonus son was already a big brother on our side and a little brother on his biological Mom's side, so he knew what it was like to have siblings. He never had the feeling of being left out because he was already involved with so much in our home concerning his younger brother. Although my middle son had his big brother with him the majority of the time, he only knew what it was like to be the baby of the house. Having to go from little brother to big brother was a big promotion and I didn't want him to feel neglected or left out once his new baby sister arrived, so I gave him a role from the time I was pregnant to after she was born. During my pregnancy, his role was to help me with small things like preparing the baby bag. We looked at baby clothes together, I allowed him to rub my belly and talk to his baby sister and we would talk about him becoming a big brother soon.

After giving birth, my daughter had to stay in NICU, so he didn't get to go straight into big brother mode. While she was in NICU I would pump breastmilk for her, so his role was to help me put the NICU label stickers on each bottle for her and to help me bag them and put them in the freezer for storage. He truly enjoyed having that role. Once our baby girl was released to come home, my middle son had to take on an even bigger role. Now he was ready to be in big brother mode; I encouraged him to help with her feedings. He would bring me bottles, I would allow him to put the scoops of milk in her bottles, he would bring me diapers and wipes when needed, and just help with her basic needs (with my assistance of course). This helped him not to feel left out and it helped him adapt to the change and to embrace the transition of no longer being the baby of the house.

Instead, he was now an amazing big brother to his new little sister. My bonus son would pitch in to help with small roles as well. It eventually got to the point where they would race to help with their baby sister. I enjoyed watching because it assured me that no one was feeling left out, neglected, or lost in their roles of being an older sibling. I said all of that to say providing roles for your child(ren) when changes are going to occur can be helpful to them. It can boost their little egos, it can give them drive, and it will encourage them to transition from one task to another task. Whether it be at home, in school, or in therapy, this is a method I found that truly helps.

Think about it, as adults we don't like to be left out of things, when it involves us, we want to know every minor detail of what is going to take place because we are participants in the change or the activity that's transpiring. That is the same respect we have to treat our child(ren) with. They may be kids, but they are human as well and we have to treat them as such. We have to include them with things that involve them not only for our children that are on the spectrum but for children in general, they have the right to know when something in their world is going to change. No, you don't have to give specific details about the event but to know that it's going to take place and when it will take place is something I feel they should be aware of.

Increasing rewards and decreasing demands is another beneficial way to help your child with changes and transitions. When I say decrease your demands what I mean is make their transition or the change less like a responsibility or chore and more fun and playful, regardless of what the task is, even if you are making a change like moving to a new place; make it fun. Find ways to get them pumped up and excited about the change. You can show them pictures of their new room and what will be in it. Additionally, highlight the fun aspects of the new house that they will enjoy once they are in it. However, be sure not to set high demands for them regarding the change or transition, as we have established that transitions and changes can be challenging for them.

Rewarding them can help decrease confusion or other behavioral problems and meltdowns. When they transition without several meltdowns or when they have adapted to a change in a fair amount of time, the reward should be instant—don't wait or hesitate. Immediately give them a snack, verbal praise, or even offer them a break to let them know they did something good and to encourage them to continue doing it. There is no better way to get your Au-some child to repeatedly do something than by rewarding them.

Mom and Dad, I don't want you to worry if your child continues to struggle with changes or transitions; this is a significant process—a big one, to be exact. They aren't going to master it overnight, and if I am honestly speaking, they may never master it, but they will learn to cope with changes and transitions. They will learn how to tolerate them more as they get older, and this is me speaking from experience.

My bonus son still struggles with major changes and sometimes small ones as well as transitioning, but each day we work on it. Each day, we use the methods we've started from day one, and we talk about it before it happens. We just do our best to help him tolerate getting from one task to another in his everyday life without several meltdowns. I can truly say the meltdowns with him have calmed down; they aren't as frequent as they used to be. But realistically speaking, they do still occur from time to time.

On this journey, you won't win all the battles, but you will see the victory come in several ways. One of the major ways you will see it will be in their progress. Our daughter still lives in meltdown city, however, we believe she will move one day. Until then, we are going to continue to help her unpack all these emotions so that when it's time to move on, she will leave with no baggage trampling behind her. Progress report city will welcome her with open arms just as it did with her big brother and just as it will or has already done for your child(ren).

Chapter 7

Consistency is Magical

Do you believe in magic? I surely do, but not the kind of magic you see in fairy tales or supernatural powers or forces. The kind of magic I'm referring to is the kind you create for your superhero. It is real, authentic, and powerful. It can change your child(ren)'s life in a matter of weeks, even days. This magic is called consistency, and it is a key factor in how your child's life evolves, the way they get through each day, and the way they handle things. Consistency involves carrying out something the same way. When there is consistency in a parent's daily actions and responses, the likelihood of your child(ren) behaving better is high. Did you know that consistency serves as an emotional security blanket for children? I didn't know it either. I quickly learned this when I became a first-time parent to my bonus son. As he grew, and as I began having children of my own, I realized that emotional security is about feeling confident and navigating the world. This includes the relationships they develop along the way. It means feeling at ease with expressing yourself, your true self, and being able to be vulnerable. Being consistent can help your child(ren) develop emotional security, which, in turn, will lessen misbehaving. Practicing consistency also helps them build trust with us as well as others. It's easy to talk about consistency and building trust, but the true test comes when you apply it to the everyday lives of you and your children. A common phrase people use is the phrase "Walk the walk"; well, my phrase is “Walking the talk”, which means practicing what you preach. If I am going to encourage others to do something, I will first implement it in my life because not only do I want my children to trust me, but I also want those around me to trust the information I am giving.

When my children and others around me trust me, it makes me feel good about what I am doing. It helps me to know that what I am doing is for the greater good of other parents, such as myself, and other children, such as my own. Consistency and hard work lead to long-term results, so walk with me into the consistency part of our journey, Moms and Dads. All these things are what your child will need as they grow, and just by giving them consistency, you are providing them with these tools. You are giving them the feeling of safety and confidence. These are so important to have, especially with children, and receiving it from your parents makes it so much more special. Think about it this way: if you cannot be consistent, you cannot make progress. If you aren't consistent with your child's routine or schedule, how can they make progress with their behavior? It's almost impossible for them to do so because they don't know what to expect each day.

There are great benefits that come with consistency. Your child's productivity will increase significantly, and they will be constantly motivated to keep going in return, and so will you. They will do better every time, meaning you will see improvement with each day that is to come. Consistency sets the guidelines, and you and your child ultimately start looking for new ways to conquer your day. Once you both gain that momentum, keep going because you are getting ready to reach the peak, and there is a breakthrough on the other side waiting. Consistency has helped my family in numerous ways.

I remember the days when my bonus son would visit with his biological Mom. He would be all over the place because he didn't have a consistent schedule while visiting her every other weekend, and he would often come back home with some behavioral issues. It would take us about a day or two to get him back on track with his weekly schedule at home. He would have a hard time in school and therapy for the first couple of days back home, but once he was able to settle, the misbehaving stopped because he then knew what to expect each day after that. That alone showed us how important it was to keep a schedule and routine in place for him. Even at the age of five, he still craves that consistency; when he doesn't get it or when his routine and daily schedules are disturbed, we are in for a wild ride. Children develop a different form of respect for their parents or any adult figure around them when they provide them with consistency and sternness. They love it when we are consistent as well as stern because they can predict how we will react.

Consistency as a parent means we do as we say we would do. Just as we desire God to be consistent with the things we pray for or the promises he gives us, our children expect the same from us because our unique children need that, no matter what. How many times have you complained about someone in your life being inconsistent? It bothered you because you wanted them to do as they said they would do; you trusted them to come through, and when they failed to do so, it resulted in disappointment.

Our children can't tell us they desire us to be consistent, but they show us through their behavior. We get disappointed by their behavior, but have you ever sought to think that they too are disappointed in us because we failed to give them a consistent routine or schedule? It doesn't mean you are failing as a parent; we all fall short on this journey. What matters is we learn something new each day and work hard to apply it so that we don't disappoint our sweet, amazing, and Au-some children. As we do that, they will work just as hard to not disappoint us. Isn't that something? We are giving and receiving all at the same time without even expecting it. Can you imagine how confusing it can be for your child(ren) when we start off being consistent, but then waver?

Imagine what can possibly be going through their mind when one week they get to play on their electronic device for the entire day without interruptions, then the next week you are telling them they can have it only for two hours. They are now in tantrum mode, upset and crying because they don't understand why they can't have it all day like last week. Or what if Mommy says, "It's okay if you don't finish your vegetables; you can be dismissed from dinner," but then another day, Dad insists, "The only way you can be excused from the table is if you finish your vegetables." Inconsistent and confusing, right? Indeed, it is! As parents, it's our job to ensure that we are on one page within our parenting as Mom and Dad. We must also ensure that nothing major changes in the way our children's routines and remain consistent as possible. When we are inconsistent with our Au-some babies this will only leave room for them to misbehave, throw tantrums, or have extreme meltdowns.

This year alone, my bonus son began having several behavioral issues in school, and we couldn't truly pinpoint why. Well, we finally realized that he had a lot of changes happening within his day-to-day at school.

He started off this school year in General Education classes, but it was over-stimulating for him, so a month in, we had a meeting to get him switched to a special education class, and he started that class as soon as possible. It was a big change for him. He met with and got accustomed to his special education teacher, but a few weeks into being in her class, getting to know her, and getting settled, there was a change to where his teacher was no longer present, and he had to have a sub – another big change for him. However, it seemed he adjusted pretty well to having a substitute teacher. They got along really well, and he adored her. His substitute teacher became his permanent teacher, but he still was having trouble in class.

His teachers, along with my husband and I, worked together to tackle what we thought was causing him to have these behavioral problems. Our son is typically a bus rider, but his Dad decided to start taking him to school some days while allowing him to ride the bus on other days. Then, his afternoon bus driver, whom he was familiar with, was out for a week or two; the substitute bus driver would be thirty-five minutes late daily during those two weeks, so he would have to go back to his special education self-contained class until the bus arrived. While waiting for his late bus, he got to play in the classroom a little longer. Well, once the original bus driver came back, he was able to go from his class straight to the bus, but he had trouble transitioning to the bus each day. In return, he would sit in the middle of the hallways, refusing to get up and go to his bus. Why? Because he wanted to go to his self-contained class and play.

All these things played a role in why he was misbehaving. He had so many changes going on that we didn't realize, but once light was shed on those changes, we immediately worked overtime to ensure that he was back on a consistent schedule. He is now doing better in his classes. He still has moments, but they aren't as severe as they were during the inconsistent shake-up. I always knew that consistency was important, but it wasn't until all these things started happening that it became even more clear to me that he had to have that; he needed it; it was vital. I am sure for so many more of our Au-some children, it is the same way, even for children who aren't on the spectrum because my middle son's days don't go right if he doesn't have that consistency. He too likes to know what is happening each day. All children must have consistency, but for our unique little ones, they need it more than you can fathom.

I want to speak a little further about being stern with your Au-some child(ren). When I say be stern with them, I don't mean yell at them, scold them, or even be mean when speaking to them. What I mean by sternness is to tell them something and not go back on your word. Yes, you may have to deepen your tone a bit when speaking to them, but not to the extent of raising your voice to yell when you talk to them. Being stern means being assertive in your authority and exercising your discipline. Some people think of it as being a negative thing simply because sternness is often confused with meanness, but they are not the same, not even close. Being stern is a positive approach to disciplining your child if it's being done correctly; it is giving direction to your child in a serious yet unwavering tone.

My children respond better to adults who are stern with them. The moment an adult wavers with them, they get off course and tend to not follow directions. They need that sternness just as they need consistency. They both go hand in hand to me because when you are both consistent with the things your child does each day as well as stern with the directions you give them throughout their day, you get better results. I am a parent who wholeheartedly believes in gentle parenting with my children. Is it always effective? Absolutely not, at least not for my children, but in those moments where my gentle parenting isn't effective, I insert my stern voice, and things get done without much of a fight from them or meltdowns.

Consistency and sternness are such powerful tools to use with your superhero because they help add to those superpowers you unlocked, and they bring them the discipline they will need to use when they go out into the world on their own. I don't want you to feel like you're doing anything wrong when you use sternness with your child(ren). Don't feel like you're doing anything wrong if you aren't knowledgeable or being consistent; this is my guide for you, Mom and Dad. This is me telling you that if you haven't tried it with your child, it's not too late to start. I always say a late start is better than no start at all. Once you start, watch how you begin to see a difference in how your child responds to you and how you begin to see a difference in their behavior.

Consistency is going to turn your child's world right side up; everything will start to make sense for them. Adding a sprinkle of sternness to the mixture will be the icing on the cake. You don't want to miss what the journey of consistency and sternness has to offer in this season of you and your child's life. So, let's get to it if you haven't already. Your babies are waiting to start this new chapter illustrated by their Au-some Mom and Dad. If you are already implementing it, job well done, Mom and Dad. Keep pushing forward with it; you are on the right track.

Chapter 8

Non-Verbal
I'm Busy Thinking

I was a bonus Mom to a non-verbal son, and I am currently a Mom of a non-verbal daughter. From my experience with both my son and daughter, I can truly say non-verbal doesn't mean our babies have nothing to say; it simply means they are busy thinking. What do I mean when I say that? I mean that although they don't have words to use, their brains are constantly on the move, and they are always busy problem-solving. I watched both of my children in amazement as they did new things and found ways to communicate with me silently. My 2-year-old is still non-verbal, but each day she does something new; she shows me new ways to listen to her and understand her wants and needs. In return, I see how she thinks and how she handles situations. When my bonus son was non-verbal, he would problem-solve effortlessly.

Our Au-some children have a unique way of communicating with us through their body language.

We don't think about it this way often, but when our children are babies and they cry, that is a form of communication; we learn to figure out what each cry means. As parents, we learn the difference between a "wet" cry and a "hungry" cry. So, with our children who are on the spectrum, we have to treat it no differently; we have to listen to learn just as we did when they were infants.

When a child throws a tantrum, it's because they want or need something, but they can't simply put it into words. When they are happy about something, they clap, shriek, or jump up and down to show excitement and happiness. That is their way of non-verbally communicating with you. I remember being so frustrated because I didn't know what my daughter needed or wanted; I couldn't figure out her tantrums. Being that this is my second go-round with an Au-some child, you would think I would have some things down packed right? But each Au-some child is different; my daughter is much more demanding than my bonus son was at her age, so it was harder with her.

I had to take a moment to watch her, almost as if I was studying her so that I could pinpoint each cry, each tantrum, and each moment of distress. It took a while, but I got it eventually, and now I am at a place where I know when she is throwing a tantrum because she just wants me to be in the same room with her while giving her space, when she is falling out about her favorite snack, when she is crying for my help with something, or even when she's crying because she doesn't want my help with something. I mastered the art of listening with more than just my ears; I now listen with my eyes and with my heart. I watched her cues, and it helped lessen my frustration. I am now in a place with my daughter where it's becoming less frustrating for her to communicate with me and less frustrating for me to understand her communication style.

My bonus son was a kid who knew how to point out things as a form of communication. My daughter is a kid who doesn't point, but she walks me to the area of the things she wants. Their communication styles are so different, even more so now than ever because my bonus son is a talker, a fluent one at that. He is still learning sentences day by day, but for the most part, he now verbally communicates, whereas my daughter is just at the stage of learning to babble. It's not consistent babble, just here and there, so I must be patient with her progress and gentle with her because she's still learning to communicate with sign language; she's mostly a body language communicator.Body language communication is the use of physical behavior, expressions, and mannerisms to communicate non-verbally; it is done more instinctively rather than consciously.

For some adults, body language communication consists of handshakes or head nods, but for children who are on the spectrum, it can consist of tantrums, crying outbursts, or grabbing your hand to lead you where they want you to go. Tantrums are viewed in a negative light, and although I am a parent who doesn't condone tantrums, I am also a parent of two Au-some children who used tantrums as a form of communication, so I understand the positive and negative sides of tantrums.

I don't encourage my child to throw tantrums to communicate with me; I am a parent who believes wholeheartedly in redirection. However, I also don't discourage her from throwing them. When I say I don't discourage it, I mean I don't get upset about her tantrums and I don't discipline the tantrums. I solely get to the root of the tantrum. Once I am at the root, I positively redirect her, introducing new ways to communicate what she was originally in tantrum mode about. I understand that she wanted to communicate something with me, and the only way she knew to do it was by communicating with her body language.

Having a non-verbal child has many challenges. We must face those challenges head-on without fear and without thinking about what those who don't, or never have had to experience what we are, have to say. I have had moments of people staring, probably thinking I need to get my toddler in check about tantrums, but they don't know or understand what I have to face or encounter day to day; they don't understand that my child is simply communicating with me in the best way she knows how. So, I block out the stares and the noise from those around me, and I zero in on what my child needs and wants. I know this has not been easy for my Au-some parents of non-verbal children, but I encourage you to focus on their body language communication with your child. Zero in on what he or she may be trying to tell you because indeed something is being said, a statement being made amid the madness. Many parents get discouraged when their child is non-verbal. I think all parents have had their own personal struggles with their child(ren) being non-verbal, and that's completely fine; I was that parent as well. When my bonus son was non-verbal, I worried extensively, but that is completely normal. Even now with my daughter, I still worry, just not as much as I did with my oldest because I've seen the outcome and progress with him, so I believe deep in my heart that my daughter will progress and begin talking as well.

Did you know that most Au-some children develop speech and become fluent speakers? That alone should give you hope for your child(ren), along with watching your child progress day to day (trust me, they will make progress); this is a Mom speaking from experience. I urge you not to stay in that place of discouragement or even frustration. Come out of that place knowing that there is hope for your child to communicate with you effectively, whether it be with words, sign language, or even positive body language communication. Keep believing that it will happen for you and your child(ren). God did amazing things for me with my bonus son; he is doing amazing things for me with my daughter, so I trust that he will do amazing things for you and your child(ren). It's not an "if it happens" type of belief; it's a "when it happens" type of belief. Keep in mind that being non-verbal isn't a hindrance for your child(ren) because their brilliant little minds are always on the move, learning new ways to communicate with Mom and Dad. Their little brains are so full of ideas and ways to problem-solve things that it's hard to even imagine. Being non-verbal means, rather, being able to communicate; your child is highly gifted in ways no one could possibly understand, sometimes in ways we as their parents can't fathom.

I am such a proud parent of a non-verbal child who communicates with me through body language. Although it's not always positive communication, she's learning, and she's communicating. So right now, at this phase, I will take what I can get from her, at least until she is able to communicate with me verbally or by signing. My heart, love, and prayers go out to each of my non-verbal Au-some Mommies and Daddies out there. All of you are amazing. No one could fill your shoes or handle those babies the way that you do. No one can understand them better than you do. So, continue to rock at being Au-some parents because your child is who they are because of you, whether they are able to tell you or not. We are often told that we should think before we speak and listen to respond. To have a child or children who have already mastered that in their younger years due to being non-verbal keeps me in awe. Our child(ren) will already go into the world with a tool that most of us don't learn to carry until we are deep into adulthood simply because they were born so Au-some. They must listen before responding due to being non-verbal, and they were born thinkers. This just further proves how Au-some their superpowers are.

Mommies and Daddies, I want you to always remember that although your non-verbal child(ren) is not a talker yet, they are thinkers, and thinkers always prosper, especially those with superpowers such as our child(ren).

Chapter 9

Verbal
I Have a Voice

I remember the day my bonus son unexpectedly said his first word. It was just another fun day at the house, and he was playing with his baby brother. They were running through the house playing, laughing, jumping on the trampoline, and just having a good time. Then, out of the blue, he got off the trampoline, ran over to me giggling, and said, "Ma." I was completely shocked. My face lit up with joy because I was so accustomed to him babbling all the time with no real words unless they were accidentally said through babble. I couldn't wrap my mind around him saying a word. I grabbed him and gave him the biggest hug. I asked if he could repeat it just to see if he knew what he said or if he could repeat it. Surely, he repeated it. At that moment, I knew he was entering the verbal stage, using words outside of babble. My heart was so full, but what made that moment more special was that it wasn't something he was taught to say. He didn't hear it from his brother because my son was calling me "Tracie", simply because that's the name he heard everyone else call me. It literally came naturally for my bonus son.

I always tell this story because it is so ironic that my bonus son started calling me mommy before my biological son did. My son started calling me mommy after hearing my bonus son say it for so long. It was such an amazing transition to see take place. It wasn't long after that first word that other words began to form effortlessly. It took time, but it seemed to me that he was learning new words quickly. He began saying "da da" and other simple words such as "hey, bye, more, no, yes". We were super proud to finally hear that beautiful little voice of his. There is something so magical about seeing your child go from non-verbal to verbal. It's a feeling that I can't quite describe; it's something that you truly must experience to understand the feeling of it. Having a voice typically means having an active and participating role in making or influencing a decision about something, but for parents of Au-some children, having a voice means so much more. It's not just about your child(ren) being able to participate in decision-making; it's more about your child being able to communicate with you in a way they weren't able to for so long.

Have you ever taught a child how to ride a bike without training wheels? It was exciting and nerve-wracking at the same time, right? I get it! Once they've fallen a couple of times, gotten back up, tried again, and mastered it, that nervous feeling you had went away and turned into pure joy and excitement for your child. Well, that's the same feeling we have as Au-some parents. We are often nervous and excited all at the same time. The nerve-wracking feeling is because they are unable to find those words; they are trying so hard, but they keep falling. But one day, out of nowhere, they fall, get up, and it happens. The words form, and now it's like clockwork. They are absorbing every new word possible, and before you know it, you have a verbal child. Now here comes that feeling of excitement; you no longer feel nervous about your child falling. All you feel now is joy and overall excitement because your child has mastered a new milestone.

Although they are just getting started, you are glad it's happening. You're not thinking about how far they have to go; you are solely thinking about how far they have come, and it feels great. Your child having a voice feels like when a person has won the lottery. You hit the jackpot! I have never won the lottery, but if I do, I'm sure it would feel exactly like this. There is so much power and joy in seeing your child master something that comes naturally to so many others. My daughter is still in her stage of being non-verbal, but I hear more sounds and unintentional words through babble, just as I did with my bonus son. I am sure that one day soon I will get to hear her beautiful voice.

It's like unwrapping a gift that has been wrapped up in multiple boxes. You are super excited about the gift, but you are also eager to get to the last box to see what the gift is. I am so eager to unlock that final superpower that I know in my heart my daughter possesses. I am excited to see her blossom into this little person who talks nonstop. I wonder what her actual voice will sound like. Will it be soft and gentle, or will it be slightly deep? I had these same questions and emotions concerning my bonus son.

I know when I finally get to that final reveal, unwrap that final box, unlock that final superpower, and get to the "Mommy I have a voice" stage, it is going to be all worth it, and that applies to each of you reading this story. You are going to be in a place that you couldn't imagine; it's going to take you by surprise, but most importantly, it's going to help you know and fully understand that you and your child's personal journey was worth the wait. It was worth every tear, every prayer, every late night, early morning. It was worth every therapy, and it was worth the exhaustion because now you are on your way to hearing your child through speaking and not just hearing them with your heart.

Do you remember your child's first word, if they had any, before they began to lose words? I do! My bonus son was saying "Dada," and my daughter was saying "Mama" and "Dada." My husband and I were the happiest parents alive in these moments of our children's lives. If you can remember this stage, you know exactly how it feels. Well, I am telling you now that feeling will resurface once your child(ren) enters back into that verbal stage. The verbal road is just the opening to the show that your child is the star of, and you are the audience. So, without further ado, I ask that you stand to your feet and begin giving your child(ren) a standing ovation because they deserve it for all of their hard work. Even if they are only at a single-word phrase level, applaud them because there is more to come. The closing act is going to have you on your toes.

Chapter 10

My Advice to You

To all my Au-some mothers and fathers out there who are dealing with an Au-some child, I encourage you to continue fighting and being the voice for your child(ren). You may get tired on this journey, and it may feel like you are at the end of your road, but I am here to tell you that YOU'RE NOT! God is walking on this journey with you, and He will not leave nor forsake you, so trust in Him and believe in yourself. God is working in your favor, and those moments of despair only last for a moment. This isn't the end for you; the journey must continue because your Au-some child(ren) depends on you. I know how tough it can be, and I understand the feeling of not knowing why you were chosen to take this journey. However, the beauty of it all is finding the strength you didn't know was there, watching your child(ren) reach those milestones that you desperately wanted to see early on, and being there to guide them every step of the way. One of my favorite quotes is "God gives His toughest battles to His strongest soldiers," and He does. I didn't realize my strength until I became a full-time bonus Mom to an Au-some bonus son. I started this journey with him, and along the way, the road got tough. I had to fight so many battles that I didn't quite understand. I questioned God numerous times, cried many nights, and lost sleep more than you could imagine. The one thing I never did was give up because I knew that God was testing my faith, strength, and my ability to trust Him even when I couldn't see the brighter side of things. We all go through different storms on this journey, but we must learn from these storms. We must continue to walk through this storm so that we can come out on the other side stronger than we were when we started this walk.

I know many of you may be familiar with the Lord's Prayer. When I'm having moments of discouragement, my go-to part of the prayer is Psalm 23:4 (KJV). It reads;

> *"Yea, though I walk through the valley of the shadow of death, I will fear no evil: for thou art with me; thy rod and thy staff they comfort me."*

That part of the prayer has so much substance. It reassures us that we shouldn't be fearful of the things that we may face as we walk on this journey because God is with us, and He will guide us through step by step, day by day. I challenge you to let the weak moments build you up and motivate you. Look at your child(ren) and allow their faces to encourage you not to waver. Don't forget how Au-some you are, Mom and Dad.

Take care of yourself. Self-care is essential; it is an absolute necessity. When you take care of yourself, you feel so much better, vibrant, and ready to conquer the world. I struggled with self-care, and if I'm being completely honest, sometimes I still find it hard to make time for myself. But as parents, in general, we must find time to breathe. Someone dear to me once told me that if I'm not good, then my child(ren) isn't good. That alone opened my eyes to taking more time for self-care because as a mother, especially an Au-some mother, I want my child(ren) to be good in every aspect.

Self-care can be numerous things, such as taking a walk to get a breath of fresh air, sitting in the sun reading a book, sitting by the pool soaking up the sun in peace, going to the gym for a good workout, sitting in your car listening to worship music, or taking yourself out to lunch to enjoy the quietness. However, you choose to take time for yourself, just make sure that you do it. Starting off, it doesn't have to be every week; you can start small and do it twice a month. Then work your way up to doing it once every other week, and eventually, it will become a habit. Before you know it, you will be unknowingly having self-care days once a week, whether it be while the children are in school, with a sitter, or late at night when they go down for bedtime. You will notice a change in how your days go; you will feel less overwhelmed and more tuned up and prepared for the day with your child(ren).

Utilize your support system. It's important, as it can alleviate a lot of stressful moments. The old saying is "It takes a village to raise a child," and it does. The village doesn't always have to be family; I learned that along the way. Your village/support system can be several people, such as the therapists that you and your child see on a weekly basis, the teachers that handle your child(ren) day to day at school or daycare, and other parents who know what you are going through on your journey. Your support system isn't and shouldn't be limited to just family and friends. The best part about having a support system that can relate to your journey is being able to unload all that you are dealing with freely, without judgment. It's vital to surround yourself with people who will listen to understand what you are struggling with, to embrace and love you through your times of hardships and through those moments of frustration. You may not know it now, but those people will be your strength, they will be your silver lining, your eye-opener, and so much more.

I can't express enough how much easier this journey became after I found my support system and actually utilized them for the needs of me and my children. I felt so uneasy in the beginning stages, not knowing who to lean on outside of my family (who also didn't know much about caring for an Au-some child because they had never embarked on this journey either), but God put people on the path of me and my children that became like family. They were more than just therapists, teachers, and doctors; they soared above their job titles and served a greater purpose in our lives. My advice to you is to welcome them with open arms and utilize them in any way possible; you don't have to carry the load alone; there are people around you ready and willing to help lift the weight of things off of you and your family. I will admit that it's not easy seeking help. As parents, we don't want to feel helpless or like we must depend on others a great deal. I want to assure you that asking for help in areas where you're experiencing things with your child(ren) although it has you at a standstill or loss of words, isn't being helpless. Remember, the end goal is to do what is necessary to help your child(ren) succeed. In doing that, we sometimes have to seek the help and advice of those around us.

Mom and Dad, you are warriors, and your child(ren) are little superheroes. A warrior is a brave or experienced soldier or fighter. You have every tool that you need to get through this journey; don't, for one second, think you aren't equipped to handle it because you are. Every obstacle that you face, you conquer it. Whether this is with tears in your eyes or sweat on your brow, you are amazing at what you do, and it shows daily. Notice how your child(ren) look at you in amazement when you haven't done much or said anything to them? That's admiration! Your child admires the hard work you put in for them; they admire the love you show even during the moments of frustration. They admire how strong-willed you are, how confident you are, how stern you are when they need it, and how brave you are day to day not knowing what the day will bring your way; that right there is WARRIOR behavior, and your child sees it in you just as I do.

Keep going, don't stop now, kings and queens, because the finish line is so close. I know you feel it, I know you can see it. There is a reward so great on the other side of this journey, and that reward is seeing your child go out into this world being the superheroes you taught them to be. They are ready to go from superhero to warrior, just like Mommy and Daddy. Pass that torch and let them light this world up with all their beautiful and Au-some colors. If no one else knows their capabilities, we as their parents know, and it's time for others to see their true colors shine through.

Acknowledgments

There have been so many things to overcome in my life, and I know that I couldn't have done it alone. I wouldn't have made it through this journey on my own. This book wouldn't be possible without my support system. I am the mother and woman I am today because I've had God, as well as these people in my life. I first would like to give God honor and praise for all He has done for me, as well as for the things He will continue to do for me on this journey and in this life. I am a woman of faith, and I couldn't be here if God didn't show His hand in my life and the lives of my children on several occasions. Even in those moments where I felt hopelessness, God was there to reassure me. He was there to lift my head, hold my hand, and walk me through each chapter of my life. God has not left my side, nor has He forsaken me, and for that, I owe Him everything. He will forever receive all the glory, praise, and honor for our victories and for our lives.

A scripture that I feel is so powerful and uplifting that will continue to bless my life is 1 Corinthians 16:13-14:

> *"Watch ye, stand fast in the faith, quit you like men, be strong. Let all your things be done with charity."*

It means be watchful, stand firm in your faith, and let all that you do be done in love. The Bible speaks about faith the size of a mustard seed and believe me when I say that is truly all that you need for God to work. My faith wavered a few times, but it never went away. I kept that mustard seed faith. God has carried me exceedingly and abundantly. Not only has He carried me, but He carried my entire family, and God, I just want to glorify your name and tell you THANK YOU!

To my amazing, hardworking, and loving husband, first, I want to thank you for giving me three of the best gifts I could possibly ask for in this life—our children. Secondly, I want to tell you how happy I am to be your wife. You are an amazing man who has supported me through everything I've set forth to do. You push me to keep going no matter what, and you encourage me to walk with my head held high. Thank you for always speaking life into me during the hardest moments of my life. Thank you for being my biggest fan in life and thank you for loving me unconditionally. Originally, I didn't see myself being a stay-at-home Mom and wife. At first, it was hard to do because I am a woman with work ethics. However, you knew our children needed me home and I trusted you. You reassured me that you would take care of our family, and you have truly kept your word. You make me a proud wife, and you make our children proud daily. I thank God for blessing me with a man who loves without fear, who desires to take care of his family—a man who is true to his family, honest, and trustworthy. Thank you for never giving me reasons to doubt you as a husband, father, or man. If I could describe you as a person in three words, it would be humble, protective, and courageous. Those are some of the qualities that drew me to you in the beginning. You are and always have been my peace, my place of rest, my best friend, and the person that I run to first, after God, when things seem to be going wrong. I love you more and more every day, and I will forever honor those vows we took on our wedding day. I wouldn't want to do life with anyone else but you.

Mom, thank you for raising me to be the woman I am today. Thank you for instilling so much love in me that I know no other way to be outside of loving. Thank you for setting boundaries, teaching me respect, and showing me that I can do anything I put my mind to. You are an amazing woman, and I appreciate all the times you shielded me from things as a child, protected me, and guided me in the direction I should go. You are my heart, and I don't want you to ever forget that. No matter what life throws at you, you overcome it. Your strength is one of the things I admire most about you, and another is how selfless you are. There has never been a moment when you didn't put your children first, and even now that we are adults, you still look out for us as well as your grandchildren. I want to honor you by giving you your flowers now. I appreciate you, and I love you more than you could ever know. Again, thank you for being an outstanding mother, the best you knew how to be.

Mama Kim, thank you for accepting me into your family. From the moment we met, you treated me like your own, greeting me with grace and love. You gave me a fair chance and never judged me. Thank you for being open to loving me as a daughter. I am eternally grateful for that; our bond grew more and more, and now we are inseparable. You are the best mother-in-love a girl could ask for, and God couldn't have handpicked a better family for me to marry into. There is never a dull moment with us. I want to let you know how much I appreciate your constant prayers, our long talks, and your encouragement with life and motherhood. I love you to pieces, and if I don't tell you enough, I am telling you now that you are loved, appreciated, and respected.

To both my mother and mother-in-love, I love you both so dearly. There is never a moment when I need either of you, and you're not there. If I call both of you, you come running, and that is such a great feeling to have. Neither of you makes me feel like I must live life alone, and that's the most important thing a mother can give to her daughter.

To all the people who stood in my corner, supported me, encouraged me, prayed for and with me, and who have loved me in spite of, I want to say I love you genuinely. I appreciate your kind words during my time of need, your jokes during my time of sorrow, your encouragement during my time of despair, and the outpour of your love during my times of heartache and uneasiness. It never went unnoticed, and I hope you felt it even when I didn't say it.

My sisters Cecily, Felicia, and Arriel, life would not be the least bit as fun or entertaining without the three of you. Each of you brings something different to my life, and although you may not know it, it's needed and always has been. I couldn't ask for a better set of "rough riders" to ride through life with. Cecily, you are the big sister who's more of a mother figure. I give you a hard time because that's my job as your little sister, but I admire the woman you are, the mother you are, and the wife you are. Let's not forget your dedication and determination to be someone in this life for yourself and your family. You are an amazing person, and I'm blessed to call you sister. Thank you for always being in my corner, whether I felt I needed you there or not; you never gave up on me, and for that, I appreciate and love you.

Felicia, I love how dedicated to Christ you are. I know that if no one else in this world is praying for me, you are. You are a beautiful soul to have around—so pure and raw all at the same time. You are who you are, and I love you for that. The mother and wife you are is unmatched. As the woman of God, you are unmatched. Our sistership is unmatched. Thank you for supporting me in every way possible. No matter what, if I call and you can help, you will be right there—no questions asked. I know you would give me the shirt right off your back because that's just how selfless you are. I love you forever, and I am glad you are my big sister.

Arriel, my pooh, you are the baby sister I never had. We are cousins by blood but sisters by heart. We have always been thick as thieves; you are my person, and you always will be my person. Thank you for always believing in me, pushing me to go harder, supporting me and my dreams, being there to listen when I need to vent, and for just overall being a great person in my life. I admire so many things about you—your mindset, your ambition, your smartness, and your willingness to persevere even when it seems like the odds are against you. You may be the little sister, but you give big sister vibes from time to time—especially in those moments when I'm driven by emotions. You are always the levelheaded one. Thank you for being calm in my storm no matter the circumstances. I love you, baby sister, and I am truly grateful to have you in my life.

To my brothers-in-law, I want to say thank you from the bottom of my heart for always being there for me. Before I was married, both of you were my protectors, and neither of you ever left me out of the equation. I was always tagging along during date nights. Thank you for always supporting me and telling me that I can do all things through Christ who strengthens me. Thank you for keeping me levelheaded and for being amazing big brothers to me. Both of you are appreciated beyond measure. I will always have a special place in my heart for you both. Each of you are amazing uncles to my children, and that alone speaks volumes. I love each of you dearly, and I can proudly say I love being able to call you BROTHER.

To my non-biological sisters, Shakia, Neeka, and Tokia, who have had my back for quite some time, I want to say that you girls are truly my day ones. You are the people I confide in most outside of my biological sisters. Having all of you in my life has been nothing short of a blessing. Sistership is to feel together, pray together, heal together, and rise together. There is no better group to do that with than each of you. You all bring something unique to my life; each personality is different but is needed. When you create bonds with other women, one of the most important things to have is a safety net, and I can truly say I have it with all of you. There is nothing I feel I must hide from you. I want to thank each one of you for being who you are, for supporting me without question, for being loyal to me as a sister. Thank you for rooting for me out loud, for having my back in my presence and behind my back, for becoming family and loving my children as you would love your own, and for keeping me in your prayers. God placed you in my life for a purpose. None of these connections happened by accident. I am grateful to not only call you friends but to call each of you, SISTER. I love you.

To Jackie Simpson, my best friend of 17 years, without a doubt you have uplifted me time and time again over the years. I can't go without telling you, thank you. Whenever I need a laugh, you are right on time. Any dream I have ever had, you encouraged me to go for it. I can't recall one time where I reached out to you for positive words, and you didn't deliver. Our friendship is one in a million. I wouldn't trade you for anything in the world. You are a great uncle to my children and an even better brother to me. You exceed the expectations of a best friend. I know that I can always count on you for encouraging words, positive views on life, prayer, support in any shape, form, or fashion, and a good laugh during moments where life seems to be unfair. I love you.

To the host of therapists and teachers that my family has encountered among both my Au-some children, I want to simply say THANK YOU! I truly can't thank each of you enough for all that you've done for my family. We are eternally grateful for each of you; you all were more than therapists and teachers to us, you were family. There was never a moment where we felt alone on this journey, and every question we had, you always answered.

Amanda Brooks, my bonus son's first early interventionist, I want to say that you went over and beyond your job for our son. You exceeded being an E.I., and you made our first experience with an E.I. the best experience ever. I don't know what we would have done without you. You didn't leave one stone unturned in our household, and we are grateful for that. Thank you for being an amazing person to our family. We love you endlessly, and I pray that your life is filled with joy, peace, and happiness because you truly deserve it.

Katherine Parker, my bonus son's second early interventionist, we are so delighted to have you. We were nervous about where we would land with therapists after our move, but surely God placed us in wonderful hands when he placed us with you. Thank you so much for always being sweet and genuine with our son, not only to Tristan but to our other two children as well. They all truly adore you, as do my husband and

I. You are another person who has yet to leave a stone unturned in our household. No matter how many questions I have, you are there to answer them to the best of your ability, and I couldn't be more grateful for that. Thank you for always reassuring me that I am doing a good job as a mother; you are always complimenting me as a parent, and it is always appreciated. You are such a beautiful soul to know, and we love having you as a part of our family. I pray an abundance of blessings upon your life, and I pray that God showers you with pure light and love daily.

Shelly Bishop, Tristan's kindergarten teacher, I want to express our deep gratitude for being a godsend to us. As a parent who values involvement in my children's education, having a teacher like you in my child's life has brought great peace to my mind and heart. Your openness to communication aligns perfectly with my own approach, and I can't overstate the ways you have assisted our family. From day-to-day interactions to helping us navigate challenges with our child, your support has been invaluable. Our son not only adores you, but we also hold you in high regard. Thank you for always being just a phone call or text away when it comes to our son. Your willingness to open your heart to the children you teach is truly commendable, especially considering the challenges of teaching children with unique abilities. Your dedication and effort stand out, and we recognize that teachers like you are rare. I pray that God continues to cover and protect you in your everyday life. May your heart's desires be fulfilled because a person of your goodness truly deserves it. Our family deeply appreciates and loves you.

An Open Letter to My Grandma

Dear Grandma,

To my late Grandmother Luella "Lil Jenny" Hutchenson, I want to thank you for helping my Mom shape and mold me into the woman I am today. You stuck by my side until the end. I can't thank God enough for lending you to me for 23 years; those were the best years of my life. You were one of the best things to happen to me in life. You taught me how to love those around me, including strangers. You taught me to give from my heart, you taught me to be grateful for all things, no matter what the circumstances may look like. You taught me to put my trust in God each and every day. Not only did you teach me these things, but you also showed me in your everyday life by doing them yourself. I learned so much just from watching you be who you were. You would give others the shirt off your back even when they have wronged you. As a little girl, as I was growing up, I didn't understand why, no matter how often you would explain it, I just couldn't see why you would still be so giving. Now, in my adult years, I understand. I often replay all those times you would say, "Baby, I can't worry about what people do or how they choose to treat me, I can only give an account for me because I have to answer to God. So, regardless of how others treat me, I will still treat them how I want to be treated. I won't miss my blessing by returning the favor of wrongdoing." That entire statement hits differently nowadays. Grandma, you were a beautiful soul and anyone who met you should count themselves lucky to have known you. You changed and influenced my life in so many ways. You guided me through some of the toughest seasons in life, but you also prepared me to do these things on my own. Thank you for giving me the tools I need to be successful in life, not just in my career but also spiritually. Thank you for loving me as much as you did. Thank you for not only being my Grandmother, but for also being my best friend. Thank you for keeping my secrets, for correcting me when I was wrong, for allowing me to have a voice, as long as that voice spoke out of respect. Thank you for raising me to walk with my head held high like the queen I am and for teaching me to love myself first. I watched you be an amazing mother and an even better Grandmother. Grandma, you would be proud to know that I am now following your lead. Your passing happened so fast and suddenly. At the time, it broke me down, but in the same token it grew me up. You always said that your prayer was to see me and my three sisters grow up and become women in this world. I am so glad you were able to see at least three out of the four of us become adults. I just want to let you know that although Pooh was a teenager when you gained your wings, she is now a beautiful woman and she turned out just fine because you raised us right and you did the same with her. I miss you lady and I love you always. This isn't "Goodbye", this is "I'll see you later! Save your baby a seat in heaven, my love!"

Sincerely,

Mama's Baby

Prayer for Parents

Father, I pray for the parents, the children, and the caregivers. I ask that you continue to bless them on this journey and cover each one of them with your love. I pray that you continue to open doors for them on this journey and strengthen a hedge of protection around them. Help them to find their way, keep them at peace as they travel on this Au-some Journey. Lord let not their hearts be troubled, God you said in your word, they that wait upon the Lord shall renew their strength; they shall mount up with wings as eagles; they shall run and not be weary and they shall walk and not faint. God help them to WAIT while on this journey, give them the patience that they need God. I ask that you order their steps in your word, teach them, and guide them daily for this battle is not theirs, it's yours. Father God, I pray that they keep that faith of a mustard seed as they continue, and I ask that you help them remember that you are with them. Lord, I want to THANK YOU for the journey, I want to thank you for keeping us even when we didn't feel kept, I want to thank you for protecting us and our babies and although we may not understand this journey we trust you and thank you for teaching us to lean not on our own understanding for you will direct our path.

In Jesus name I pray,

AMEN!

About the Author

Tracie Green, 32, was born in Chicago, IL and raised in Indianola, Ms. She now resides in Greer, SC with her husband and their three beautiful children. She's the youngest of four children. She was inspired by her children to write this book as a testament of hope, faith, and love. She enjoys being in peaceful environments and helping other Mothers and Fathers that are on the same walk of life as she and her husband. She is a woman of good faith, strength, ambition, independence, inner beauty, and grace. Matthew 5:5 tells us, "Blessed are the meek, for they will inherit the earth." Tracie is living proof of a meek and humble woman.

Stay connected with Tracie on social media today!

TikTok @ tristankamtink_mommy

FB @ Tracie Monquie

Printed in Great Britain
by Amazon

48666796R00066